The Boeing B-47 Strat

A Photographic History

by Mark Natola

Schiffer Military History
Atglen, PA

Dedication

This book is dedicated to the men who designed, flew and maintained the Boeing B-47 Stratojet throughout the darkest days of the Cold War.

Special thanks go to the following individuals, without whose assistance this book would not have been possible: Robert M. Robbins, James Fraser, Raymond McPherson, William Campbell, Russ Schleeh, George Birdsong, Sigmund Alexander, Tom Sams, Jack Martin, Mike Pulchney, Skip Ulring, Jack Reading, Robert Loffredo, David Hall, Robert Dorr, Ken Miner, Clifford Goodie, Paul Houser, Stan Flenjti, Jack Kovacks, Bruce Bailey, Joseph Bauer, Charles Anderson and Mike Habermehl.

Cover Photos
The Boeing XB-47 Stratojet medium bomber flies over the Cascade mountain range during Phase I flight testing.

Rear Cover
A B-47 refueling with a KC-97 Stratotanker.

Book design by Ian Robertson.

Copyright © 2010 by Mark Natola.
Library of Congress Control Number: 2010939006

Printed in China.
ISBN: 978-0-7643-3758-1

We are interested in hearing from authors with book ideas on related topics.

Published by Schiffer Publishing Ltd.
4880 Lower Valley Road
Atglen, PA 19310
Phone: (610) 593-1777
FAX: (610) 593-2002
E-mail: Info@schifferbooks.com.
Visit our web site at: www.schifferbooks.com
Please write for a free catalog.
This book may be purchased from the publisher.
Please include $5.00 postage.
Try your bookstore first.

In Europe, Schiffer books are distributed by:
Bushwood Books
6 Marksbury Avenue
Kew Gardens
Surrey TW9 4JF, England
Phone: 44 (0) 20 8392-8585
FAX: 44 (0) 20 8392-9876
E-mail: Info@bushwoodbooks.co.uk.
Visit our website at: www.bushwoodbooks.co.uk
Try your bookstore first.

Contents

Introduction

On December 17, 1947, coincidentally the 44th anniversary of the Wright Brothers' historic first flight at Kitty Hawk, Boeing experimental test pilots Robert M. Robbins and Scott Osler made the initial flight in the all jet, swept wing, Boeing XB-47 Stratojet medium bomber. The uneventful flight from Boeing Field, Seattle, to the Moses Lake Army Airfield in central Washington lasted just 52 minutes. As Robbins would later recall, "My job that day was to get it up and to get it down unharmed." In so doing, he and Osler ushered in the era of modern jet travel.

The genesis of the B-47 began in 1943 when, fearing the fall of Europe to the Germans, the U.S. Army Air Forces put out a request for an all jet bomber capable of flying 3,500 nautical miles. Ed Wells, then Boeing's chief engineer, instructed Bob Jewett, chief of preliminary design, to begin working on such an aircraft. In 1944, a revised request for proposals for an aircraft capable of flying up to 1,000 nautical miles at 500 mph at an altitude of at least 40,000 feet was issued.

During the closing days of World War II in Europe, Boeing's chief aerodynamicist, George Schairer, accompanied the renowned scientist Theodor von Karman on a tour of captured German industrial facilities. Writing to Boeing's Ben Cohn, Schairer described German technical advances in aerodynamics, including preliminary design work utilizing swept wing technology. Although Schairer's letter was greeted with interest at Boeing, straight wing designs would continue to dominate the aviation industry.

By the end of the war, advances in jet engine technology would lead to several all jet bomber designs, including the North American XB-45, the Convair XB-46, the Martin XB-48, and the Northrop YB-49 Flying Wing. With the exception of the YB-49, each aircraft featured pod mounted jet engines hung below the leading edges of the wings. Although flying characteristics varied, none of the designs proved to be a breakthrough, and only the Martin XB-45 would go into production with 143 aircraft being built, most serving in the reconnaissance role.

Boeing's initial entry in the all jet bomber competition was the Model 424, which owed much to its predecessor, the B-29. Like the others, the Model 424 sported four pod mounted jet engines suspended beneath the leading edge of conventional straight wings. NACA (National Advisory Committee for Aeronautics) wind tunnel tests on the Model 424 demonstrated that the engine layout created excessive drag and the design was rejected. With the Model 432, Boeing removed the engines from the wings and placed them inside the fuselage, a decision rejected by the Army Air Force, who feared the results of a catastrophic engine failure.

Following the rejection of the Model 432 Boeing produced the Model 448, which featured both swept wings and tail surfaces, and an additional pair of fuselage mounted engines. Once again the concept of internal engines was rejected and Boeing engineers returned to the drawing board. Finally, with the Model 450, the engines were removed from the fuselage and suspended from streamlined pylons below the swept wings. This design not only reduced drag, but offered improved safety in the event of engine malfunction.

By the spring of 1946, as Boeing prepared to build the B-50A Superfortress, essentially an upgraded version of the B-29 featuring four 3,500 hp Pratt and Whitney R-4360-35 Wasp Major radial engines, the pinnacle of piston engine technology, a letter contract for two XB-47 prototype aircraft was received. Few outside of the B-47 design team could have imagined that the Stratojet's revolutionary design would make all current aircraft, including the B-50, obsolete when it took to the skies in December 1947.

With a wing sweep of 35-degrees, a sleek fuselage, forward mounted engine nacelles, tandem bicycle-style landing gear and outrigger wheels, the Stratojet was a radical departure from its contemporaries. The first XB-47, 46-065, would utilize six General Electric J-35-GE-7 axial flow turbojet engines rated at 4,000 lbs. thrust each and could be fitted with eighteen 1,000 lb. thrust jettisonable rockets for RATO takeoffs.

The second aircraft, 46-066, featured upgraded General Electric J-47-GE-3 axial flow turbojet engines capable of 5,200 lbs thrust each and featured many enhancements. With a top speed of nearly 600 mph, the B-47 bomber was as fast as the newest fighters then under development, and therefore required little more than a pair of tail guns for protection.

Despite the initial excitement generated by the XB-47, the newly created United States Air Force maintained that the conventional Boeing B-50 was the bomber of the future. However, during a scheduled visit with Boeing's president Bill Allen in Seattle in July 1948 where they were to discuss B-50 production, General K. B. Wolfe, the head of Air Force bomber production, was convinced to stop at Moses Lake to evaluate the XB-47, which was undergoing Phase II flight testing. Upon his arrival at Moses Lake, Colonel Pete Warden, "the Father of the B-52," recommended that General Wolfe accompany Air Force test pilot Major Guy Townsend on an orientation flight in the XB-47. Having never flown in a jet before, General Wolfe agreed. Following the demonstration flight, Major Townsend made a low, high-speed pass across the air field, culminating with a dramatic pull up before the assembled onlookers. Within a week General Wolfe had placed an order for the first ten B-47A production model aircraft.

In January 1951, the Air Force accepted the first B-47B model aircraft into the inventory. By the time B-47 production ended in 1956, a combined total of 2,032 Stratojets had been built by the Boeing, Lockheed, and Douglas aircraft companies. With more than 25 variants, the B-47 airframe was the backbone of the Strategic Air Command throughout the 1950s. By the 1960s, however, the B-47 was being phased out in favor of the superior Boeing B-52 Stratofortress.

The last operational flight of a United States Air Force B-47 occurred on October 30, 1969, when a WB-47E, 51-7066, belonging to the 55th Weather Reconnaissance Squadron, was flown from McClellan Field to Boeing Field in Seattle, WA. Two B-47s, known as NUCAR-3 and NUCAR-4, remained in service with the United States Navy throughout the 1970s for use in fleet electronic warfare testing. The final flight of any B-47 occurred on June 17, 1986, when General John J.D. Moore and Colonel Dale Wolfe flew a restored B-47E, 52-0166, from the China Lake Naval Air Station, where it had served as a radar target to the museum at Castle Air Force Base in California.

Chapter 1:
Design and Development of the XB-47

In September 1943, Boeing's Chief Engineer, Ed Wells, instructed Bob Jewitt, then Chief of Preliminary Design, to work up a jet bomber. *Bob Robbins*

"The Flying Guinea Pig" at Boeing Field, Seattle, in September 1942 prior to its first flight. Note the three bladed props and pitot static tube on top of the vertical fin and lack of turrets. *Bob Robbins*

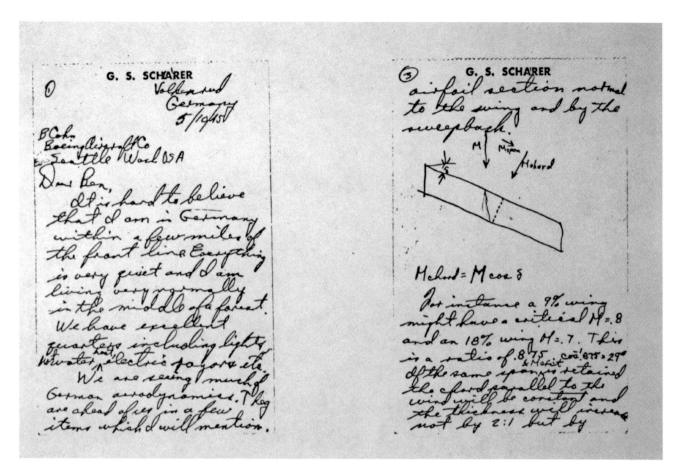

George Schairer's 10 May 1945 letter describing German swept wing technology. *Bob Robbins*

Boeing engineer George Schairer. *Bob Robbins*

Utilizing a conventional WW II wing design and tricycle landing gear, Martin's XB-45 first flew on March 17, 1947. *Bob Robbins*

Bottom: The XB-45 was powered by four Allison J-35-A-11 turbojet engines which suffered from poor acceleration. *Bob Robbins*

By the time the Convair XB-46 took to the air on April 2, 1947, the Army Air Forces had already selected the XB-45 as its first all jet bomber. *Bob Robbins*

With a crew of three, the XB-46 proved to be underpowered and incapable of meeting the requirements set forth by the Army Air Forces. *Bob Robbins*

The Martin XB-48 first flew on June 22, 1947, and it featured six J-35 turbojet engines. *Bob Robbins*

Due to the thin wing design, the XB-48 utilized bicycle landing gear and outrigger wheels similar to the XB-47. *Bob Robbins*

Two radial engined Northrop YB-35 Flying Wings were converted to utilize eight J-35 turbo jet engines. *Bob Robbins*

The first flight of the # 1 YB-49 occurred on October 21, 1947. *Bob Robbins*

The Boeing B-50A Superfortress borrowed much from its predecesor, the B-29. Modifications included upgraded 3,500 hp Pratt & Whitney R4360 radial engines and a taller vertical stabilzer. *Bruce Bailey*

In 1946, the Army Air Force had selected the B-50 as the next generation of medium bomber design. *Bruce Bailey*

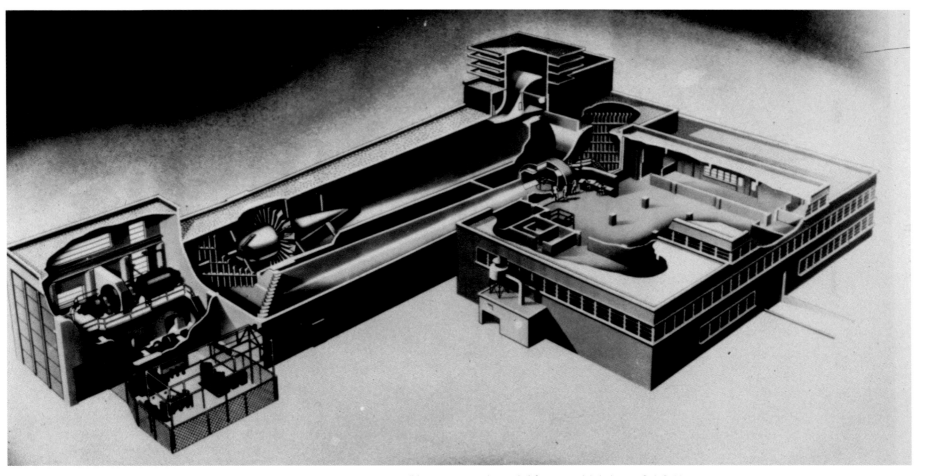

The wind tunnel at Boeing made it possible to test experimental airframe models in house. *Bob Robbins*

Boeing aerodynamicist Bob Withington was responsible for conducting wind tunnel testing on the XB-47. *Bob Robbins*

The evolution of the B-47 design can be seen in this series of wind tunnel models featuring, from left to right, the model 424, model 432 and the model 450. *Bob Robbins*

The B-47 design group at Boeing. *Bob Robbins*

The B-47 flutter model in the Boeing wind tunnel.
Bob Robbins

Technicians from Boeing's Engineering Mechanical Laboratory review flutter model test data. *Bob Robbins*

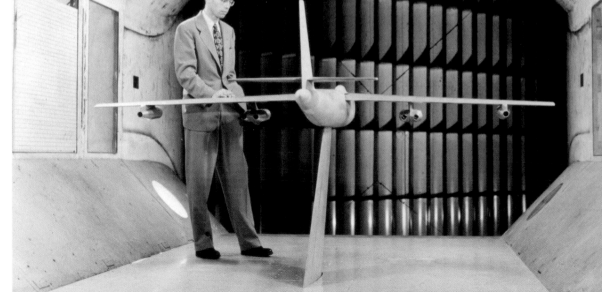

Boeing's Lloyd Goodmanson prepares the B-47 model for wind tunnel testing. *Bob Robbins*

The B-47 flutter model undergoes wind tunnel testing. *Bob Robbins*

The Boeing B-47 design team (L - R) George Shairer, Ed Wells, George Martin, Bob Jewett and model. *Bob Robbins*

The empennage for the #2 XB-47 with elevator and rudder control was tested in the Moffat (Ames) Field wind tunnel. *Bob Robbins*

The Martin B-26 "Middle River Stump Jumper" outfitted with bicycle landing gear and outrigger wheels later utilized on the B-47. *Bob Robbins*

Flight crew of the #2 XB-29 "The Flying Guinea Pig" Moses Lake AAB, Washington, June 1945. Standing (R to L) Bob Robbins- pilot, Don Whitworth- lead flight test engineer, Ernie Code- copilot, Ben Head- flight engineer, H. Washburn- radio operator, Bob Britton- flight test engineer. *Bob Robbins*

44,000 foot research work in the B-29 on 2/15/46. From (L to R) copilot Bob Robbins, project flight test engineer Ben Werner, and flight test project pilot Jim Fraser (later the copilot during the XB-47 Phase III test phase). *Bob Robbins*

Bob Robbins in the Link Trainer along with Harry Cramer. *Bob Robbins*

A B-50 test bed aircraft was fitted with a trapeze mounted TG-180 turbojet engine that could be lowered into the airstream and operated in flight. The engine tests were the only TG-180 flight experience prior to the first flight of the XB-47. *Bob Robbins*

Boeing XB-47 Project Test Pilots Robert "Bob" Robbins (in the cockpit) and Scott Osler checking out a P-80 prior to JATO testing at Muroc. *Bob Robbins*

Robbins and Osler reviewing the JATO system of the P-80. *Bob Robbins*

A volunteer awaits launch in the ejection seat rig at Wright-Patterson AFB. *Bob Robbins*

The ejection seat rig from 70 feet. *Bob Robbins*

Pilots Bob Robbins and Scott Osler sporting specially made Lombard crash helmets. Unfortunately, the gold painted helmets did not save Scott Osler during an in-flight canopy malfunction. *Bob Robbins*

Chapter 2:
Roll Out and First Flight of the XB-47

Roll out of the #1 XB-47 (46-065) at Boeing Field on 12 September 1947 to minimal fanfare as Boeing workers look on. *Bob Robbins*

The sleek lines of the radical XB-47 are evident as it is towed from the hangar at Boeing Field. *Bob Robbins*

The future meets the past as Boeing's new "Stratojet" medium bomber is towed past a partially assembled B-50 on the ramp at Boeing Field. *Bob Robbins*

Boeing experimental test pilots Bob Robbins and Scott Osler are all smiles at the roll out of the XB-47. *Bob Robbins*

Bob Robbins beneath the XB-47. Note the rope ladder hanging from the entry hatch. "Boeing made great airplanes, but they couldn't make a boarding ladder that worked." *Bob Robbins*

Pilots Scott Osler and Bob Robbins chatting with Boeing's N.D. Showalter. *Bob Robbins*

Robbins and Osler in the cockpit with the unique clamshell canopy open.
Bob Robbins

Robbins prepares for the initial take off roll on 17 December 1947, coincidentally the 40th anniversary of the Wright Brothers' first flight at Kitty Hawk. *Bob Robbins*

The first flight of the XB-47. "My overriding first flight objective was to get it up and get it down undamaged!" *Bob Robbins*

Following an uneventful 52-minute maiden flight, the XB-47 taxis at Moses Lake Airfield, WA. *Bob Robbins*

Robbins and Osler enjoying the post-flight press conference. Bob Robbins describes the XB-47's flight handling characteristics as "Good." *Bob Robbins*

The Boeing hangar at Moses Lake, AFB. *Bob Robbins*

Ed Pfafman fills the coal stove at the Moses Lake barracks.
Bob Robbins

"The conditions at Moses Lake were primitive." *Bob Robbins*

The XB-47 undergoes routine maintenance in the Moses Lake hangar. *Bob Robbins*

Test Pilot Chuck Yeager and Bob Robbins following their flight. *Bob Robbins*

Chapter 3:
Flight Testing the XB-47

USAF brass and Boeing executives gather following Maj. General K. B. Wolfe's (far left) 26-minute orientation flight with Major Guy Townsend (second from right) on 19 July, 1948, at Moses Lake. *Guy Townsend*

Air Force test pilot Major Guy M. Townsend and Bob Robbins chatting under the XB-47. Townsend flew the USAF Phase II flight test program on the #1 XB-47 from July through August 1948. *Bob Robbins*

The XB-47 reaching altitude during a JATO assisted take off. *Guy Townsend*

JATO provided an additional 18-thousand pounds of thrust for the underpowered GE J-35 jet engine. *William Campbell*

An unassisted take off. *George Birdsong*

General Curtis Lemay discussing the XB-47 program with Major Guy Townsend. *William Campbell*

Boeing Experimental Test Pilot James Fraser seated in the cockpit of the XB-47 at Moses Lake, winter 1948. *James Fraser*

XB-47 Phase III Project Pilots Scott Osler and Jim Fraser in the cockpit prior to the in-flight canopy accident which later killed Osler. *James Fraser*

XB-47 walk around, left front 3/4 view of the #1 aircraft. *William Campbell*

Left rear 3/4 view of the #1 XB-47. *William Campbell*

Rear view of the #1 XB-47 demonstrates the preproduction tail cone. *William Campbell*

The XB-47 during drag chute landing tests at Moses Lake. The test program was overseen by the German technician who helped develop the parachute for the JU-87 Stuka dive bomber in WWII. *James Fraser*

Jim Fraser and Scott Osler chatting with the base commander at Moses Lake, WA, mid-1948 with the XB-47 #2 and an F-82 in the background. James Fraser

An early publicity shot of the XB-47 taken near Moses Lake, WA, in 1948. *James Fraser*

Publicity photo of the XB-47 used in numerous advertisements promoting the Air Force's newest jet bomber. *James Fraser*

An overhead shot of the XB-47 taken during Phase III flight testing. *James Fraser*

XB-47s one and two inside the hangar at Moses Lake. *Bob Robbins*

The number two XB-47 (s# 46-066) during a dramatic JATO takeoff from Moses Lake. *Bob Robbins*

Boeing Test Pilot Tex Johnston (2nd from left) and the #2 XB-47. *Bob Robbins*

Air Force Test Pilots Majors Joseph Howell and Russ Schleeh and Boeing's Scott Osler planning the route to Andrews AFB, where they would join up with B-45, the XB-49, and the F-86 for a presidential and congressional review. *Russ Schleeh*

Schleeh, Osler, and Howell reviewing the checklist prior to takeoff from Moses Lake. *Russ Schleeh*

Majors Schleeh and Howell sporting "Wonder bread" helmets prepare for takeoff. Pilot Schleeh had a one-hour orientation flight prior to the mission. *Bob Robbins*

Major Schleeh peers from the cockpit of the XB-47 prior to takeoff. *Russ Schleeh*

Major Schleeh landing the XB-47 at Andrews AFB, Washington D.C., after setting the "unofficial" transcontinental speed record with an elapsed time of three hours and forty-six minutes from Moses Lake, WA, in 1949. *Russ Schleeh*

Your $3.65 Is Needed—Give the Red Cross at Least a Penny a Day

Boeing Plane Talk

VOL. VII   WICHITA, KANSAS, FRIDAY, FEBRUARY 18, 1949   NO. 3

RED CROSS DRIVE OPENS TUESDAY MORNING

Stratojet Smashes Air Speed Record

Plant Campaign To be Conducted By Pledge Cards

Boeing-Wichita's nearly 8,000 employees will join together in behalf of one of the nation's most worthy causes next week. On Tuesday and Wednesday, February 22 and 23, the 1949 campaign to raise funds for the American Red Cross will be held here in the plants.

The drive will actually get under way Monday, February 21, with a series of meetings to be attended by all foremen. George Gow, news editor of Radio Station KFH and an enthusiastic backer of Red Cross activities, will speak at these meetings on the functions and needs of the organization.

The first meeting will be held at 9 a.m. in the conference room in the Personnel building for all first shift foremen at Plant II.

Second at Plant I

At 10 a.m. the second meeting, to be attended by first shift foremen at Plant I, will get under way in the Personnel conference room in the Plant I tunnel.

At 7 p.m. Monday, the last meeting, for *all* second shift foremen from both plants, will be held in the Personnel building conference room at Plant II.

Pledge cards for payroll deductions have been made out so that every employee may have the opportunity of

The February 18, 1949, edition of Boeing Plane Talk declares, "Stratojet Smashes Air Speed Record." The average speed of 607.8 miles per hour broke all coast to coast speed records.
Russ Schleeh

Chapter 4:
The Production Aircraft

The B-47A

The Air Force issued a contract to Boeing on November 22, 1948, for an initial order of ten B-47A model aircraft, all to be built at the Wichita, Kansas, facility. The number one aircraft, #91900, first flew on June 25, 1950. *Bob Robbins*

The ten B-47A model aircraft were essentially service test versions of the XB-47s. Similarities to the two prototypes can be seen in this in-flight view of aircraft #91900. *Bob Robbins*

The B-47A was powered by six J47-GE-11 turbojet engines, each capable of up to 5,200 lbs of thrust. Left side view of aircraft #91905 during takeoff from Wright-Patterson AFB. *William Campbell*

Due to sluggish engine response times and braking issues in early model aircraft a jettisonable 16-foot drogue parachute and a 32-foot deceleration chute, both located beneath the tail, were deployed prior to landing. The drogue chute, which was designed by the same German engineer responsible for the Ju-87 Stuka dive-bomber's chute system, could be jettisoned in the event of a go-around at high speed. This photo shows the second production model aircraft, #91901, with the 32-foot parachute deployed. *William Campbell*

The B-47A entered service with the 306th Bomb Wing at MacDill AFB in May 1951. Although they were delivered without essential systems, such as bomb-nav equipment and tail armament, they were utilized for air and ground crew training. Aircraft #91904 demonstrates the framed nose cone of the "A" model, one of the few outward changes from the prototype aircraft. Static dischargers can be seen hanging from the wings, as well as the original XB-47 design rectangular crew entry hatch. *Jack Martin*

The final "A" model aircraft, #91909, flies alongside a North American F-86 Sabre jet. North American utilized the same captured German swept wing technology employed on the B-47 in their design of the F-86. *William Campbell*

The B-47B

Although originally scheduled to be manufactured by Boeing at the Wichita plant, increased B-47B production needs required additional facilities at the Douglas and Lockheed plants. A total of 399 B-47Bs were built between March 1951 and June 1953. Outward changes, such as a faired nose section, the K-2 periscopic bomb sight, and a newly designed crew entry hatch can be seen in this photograph. *William Campbell*

In an effort to save weight ejection seats, which had been incorporated into the B-47A design, were removed from all B-model aircraft; they were, however, retrofitted to all aircraft during the "Ebb Tide" and "High Noon" upgrade programs beginning in 1953. The ramp at Boeing Field Seattle is lined with B-29, B-50 and C-97 aircraft as this "B" model undergoes inspection. *Bob Robbins*

Original plans called for the B-47B to receive the tail mounted Emerson A-2 defensive armament system. Concerns with the Emerson system, however, resulted in the General Electric A-5 system being selected. Many B-47Bs were delivered with the tapered tail cones until defensive armaments were fitted. *Bob Robbins*

The B-47B was delivered with six General Electric J-47-GE-11 engines and the 18-bottle internal JATO system, and was capable of carrying up to 18,000 lbs of conventional or nuclear weapons. This underside view demonstrates the internal fuselage mounted JATO system and the redesigned vertical stabilizer. *Bob Robbins*

The first B-47B was accepted by the Air Force in March 1951. A total of ten B-model aircraft were assembled by Douglas at Tulsa and eight more by Lockheed at the Marietta plant utilizing parts supplied by Boeing. A badge above the cockpit entry door identifies this "B" model aircraft as belonging to the Air Force Flight Test Center. *William Campbell*

The B-47B was the first Stratojet to be fitted with an air-to-air refueling receptacle. In-flight refueling allowed the medium range B-47 to become a truly intercontinental bomber. *William Campbell*

Beginning with the 89th built aircraft, the B-47B received the upgraded General Electric J47-GE-23 engine, which was capable of 5,800 lbs of thrust. Eventually, all B-model aircraft would be upgraded with the new engine. The throttle column of a B-47B. *Mike Pulchney*

The 306th Bomb Wing at MacDill took delivery of the first B-47B in June 1951. A 306th based B-47B prepares for take-off from MacDill. *Ray McPherson*

As originally configured, the B-47-B utilized an 18-bottle internally mounted JATO system. Eventually all B-model aircraft would have this system removed in favor of the external rack mounted system used in late production aircraft. *Skip Ulring*

The North American F-86 Sabre utilized the same swept wing technology as the B-47. Here, an F-86 flies inverted alongside a B-47B. The elongated engine inlets of the early model aircraft are clearly seen. *William Campbell*

A B-47B #51-2047 of the ARDC with a canvas boot covering the nose section. Note the lengthened bomb bay doors. *Jack Martin*

The B-47E

1341 B-47E model aircraft were produced by the Boeing, Douglas and Lockheed aircraft companies, making it the largest production variant. *Mike Pulchney*

The B-47E utilized six General Electric J-47-GE-25 engines, each capable of 7200 pounds of thrust with water injection. *Bob Loffredo*

Ejection seats, which had been deleted in the B-47B series of aircraft, were reintroduced in the B-47E. Numerous modifications were incorporated in the B-47E design, including the deletion of the Plexiglas windows in the Bomb/Nav compartment and redesigned engine nacelles. *Ken Miner*

Several variations of the reflective white "anti-flash" paint scheme were utilized. As can be seen in this photograph, all under surfaces, including nacelles, pylons, and most of the fuselage were painted. *Tom Sams*

Following page: This standard configuration "E" model, complete with wing tanks, flies high above Lockbourne AFB. *Cliff Goodie*

B-47E deliveries began in February 1953, and by 1956 the Stratojet made up 29 medium bomb wings. *Cliff Goodie*

The unrefueled combat radius of the B-47E was greater than 2,000 miles; however, aerial refueling with the KC-97 Stratotanker made the B-47 a truly intercontinental bomber. *Cliff Goodie*

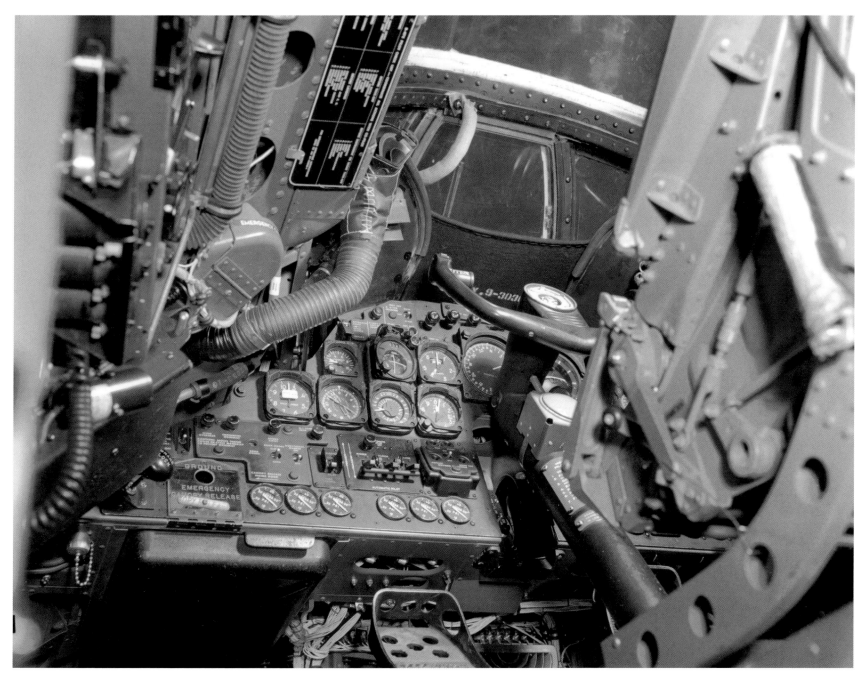

The pilot's cockpit as seen from the narrow walkway below. *Bob Robbins*

The 18-bottle internal JATO system of the previous models was replaced on the B-47E with a jettisonable 33-bottle "Horse Collar" unit. Each bottle provided 1,000 pounds of additional thrust for 10-seconds during heavy weight take-offs. *Bob Robbins*

The horse collar rack is clearly seen in this photo without the bottles installed. *Bob Robbins*

A dramatic JATO takeoff. *Ray McPherson*

The B-47E received the long awaited A-5 fire control system, which was capable of tracking approaching aircraft and firing a pair of 20 mm tail mounted cannons controlled by the A-5 fire control system. *Tom Sams*

The 1,000ᵗʰ Witchita-built Stratojet

The 1,000th Wichita-built B-47, aircraft # 52-609, emerges from the final assembly hangar to considerable fanfare on 14 October, 1954. *Paul Houser*

Boeing employees covered the 1,000th aircraft with graffiti and more than $12,000 in cash during a March of Dimes fund drive. *Paul Houser*

The 1,000th B-47 Stratojet medium bomber built by Boeing's Wichita Division is shown high over Kansas during a test flight. Accompanying the plane is # 1,001, an RB-47E. *William Campbell*

Captain Paul Houser, Pilot of the 1,000th aircraft, and his wife, Patty, are joined by Boeing Senior Project Engineer and former XB-47 test pilot Bob Robbins at Smokey Hill AFB on 17 December, 1954, exactly 7 years to the day after Robbins' first flight in the XB-47. *Paul Houser*

B/G Sutherland, Captain Paul Houser, Ms. Donna Lindsey, L/G Sweeney, and Colonel Burns at the official christening of "City of Salina" Wichita built B-47 December 17, 1954, at Smokey Hill AFB. *Paul Houser*

"Photo-Reconnaissance," the RB-47E

240 RB-47E photo-reconnaissance aircraft were built by Boeing-Wichita. Changes from the basic B-47E model included an elongated glassed nose, installation of up to 11 cameras, and the elimination of bombing equipment. In this photo the second Wichita built RB-47E flies alongside a B-47E. *Bob Robbins*

The internal fuel capacity of the RB-47E was increased to allow extended flight times for photographic missions. The ground crew stands by as the flight crew completes preflight checklist. *Cliff Goodie*

At the height of the Cold War, RB-47Es regularly probed and occasionally penetrated Soviet airspace in daring photo-recon missions. *Stan Flejenti*

Opposite: Overhead view of an RB-47E. *Bob Robbins*

"Electronic Surveillance," the RB-47H

The RB-47H was a reconnaissance and electronic countermeasures aircraft flown by the 55th Strategic Reconnaissance Wing based at Forbes AFB, Kansas. *Bob Robbins*

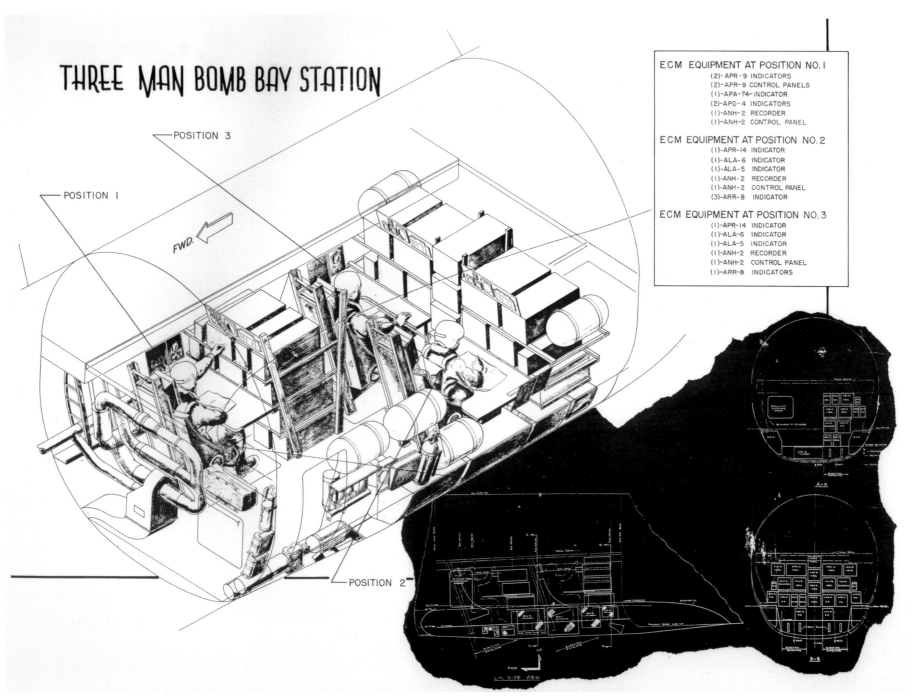

THREE MAN BOMB BAY STATION

POSITION 3

POSITION 1

FWD.

POSITION 2

ECM EQUIPMENT AT POSITION NO.1
(2)-APR-9 INDICATORS
(2)-APR-9 CONTROL PANELS
(1)-APA-74-INDICATOR
(2)-APD-4 INDICATORS
(1)-ANH-2 RECORDER
(1)-ANH-2 CONTROL PANEL

ECM EQUIPMENT AT POSITION NO.2
(1)-APR-14 INDICATOR
(1)-ALA-6 INDICATOR
(1)-ALA-5 INDICATOR
(1)-ANH-2 RECORDER
(1)-ANH-2 CONTROL PANEL
(3)-ARR-8 INDICATOR

ECM EQUIPMENT AT POSITION NO.3
(1)-APR-14 INDICATOR
(1)-ALA-6 INDICATOR
(1)-ALA-5 INDICATOR
(1)-ANH-2 RECORDER
(1)-ANH-2 CONTROL PANEL
(1)-ARR-8 INDICATORS

Three "Crows" flew inside a pressurized Electronic Counter Measures (ECM) capsule filled with electronics equipment and located in the bomb bay. *Bob Robbins*

RB-47H reconnaissance missions were highly classified and often involved penetration of Soviet airspace. Several encounters with Soviet and North Korean defenders resulted in aircraft being shot down or damaged beyond repair. *Bob Robbins*

The RB-47H sported numerous antennas, pods and sensors which housed various ELINT equipment. *Bob Robbins*

Due to the enlarged radome of the "H" model, the nose mounted refueling receptacle of the bomber was modified and placed closer to the wind screen. *Bob Robbins*

An RB-47H with an F-111 radome attached, 53-4296, was utilized by the Air Force Avionics Laboratory as a flying test bed for the F-111 radar system. *Bob Robbins*

"Photo-Weather Recon," the RB-47K

Operated by the 55th Strategic Reconnaissance Wing at Forbes AFB, 15 Wichita-built RB-47Es received side-looking radar equipment which enabled them to conduct both photographic and weather reconnaissance missions. *Bob Robbins*

In addition to gathering weather information, RB-47Ks were deployed to bases around the world where they would conduct air sampling following Soviet and Chinese above ground nuclear tests. *Bob Robbins*

"Tell-Two," the EB-47TT

Three EB-47E (TT) "Tell-Two" aircraft, modified B-47Es, were used to collect telemetry data near Soviet ballistic missile launch sites. This photo demonstrates the original configuration paddle antennas. *Jack Kovacks*

The "Tell-Two" aircraft of the 55th Strategic Reconnaissance Wing were based in Incirlic, Turkey. Aircraft # 03-2315 is seen with late model Tell-Two antennas installed. *Bruce Bailey*

"Weather Recon," the WB-47B and WB-47E

Following the hurricane season of 1954, a single B-47B, # 51-2115, was modified to perform weather reconnaissance and other duties. "Sweet Marie" sported a variety of colorful paint schemes until it was retired in favor of converted B-47Es in the early 1960s. *Sigmund Alexander*

The WB-47Es of the 9th Weather Reconnaissance Wing at McClellan AFB, CA, and Ramey AFB, PR, were used in a variety of weather reconnaissance roles. Several WB-47s were reportedly used during the "Arc Light" operations in Vietnam, making them the only known B-47s to have actively participated in the Vietnam War. *Bob Robbins*

The Ramey AFB WB-47Es were used as "Hurricane Hunters" for several years until they were replaced by the WC-130. *Bob Robbins*

An environmentalist's nightmare; a WB-47E utilizes water injection during take-off. *Jack Reading*

The final flight of a WB-47E occurred on 24 October, 1969, when the last operational B-47 in the US Air Force inventory, aircraft # 51-2390, was flown from the Douglas maintenance facility at Tulsa, Oklahoma, to Davis Monthan, AFB. With no fanfare, # 51-2390 is seen here prior to take-off for the boneyard at Davis Monthan AFB. *Bob Robbins*

"Turbo Props," the XB-47D

In 1951 the Air Force awarded Boeing a contract to evaluate the feasibility of turboprop engines. Boeing modified two B-47B airplanes (# 51-2103 and 51-2046) to serve as test beds for the Curtis-Wright YT-49 turboprop engine. *Ray McPherson*

The YT-49-W-1 turboprop engine was based on the British designed Saphire axial flow turbojet. Wright added a reduction gear for the propeller and a third turbine. *Ray McPherson*

The YT-49 engines of the XB-47D were capable of 9710 shaft horse power and drove 15' diameter 4-bladed Curtis Electric propellers with automatic feathering and ground reversing. *Ray McPherson*

Although there were numerous delays in the XB-47D flight test program, the first flight of aircraft # 51-2103 occurred on August 26, 1955. *Ray McPherson*

Boeing Experimental Test Pilots Ray McPherson and Lew Wallick congratulate each other following the first successful flight of the XB-47D. *Ray McPherson*

The second airframe, # 51-2146, in flight. The handling characteristics of the XB-47D were similar to the B-47B throughout the flight envelope. *Ray McPherson*

The XB-47D utilized the same in-flight refueling system as production model aircraft. *Ray McPherson*

Although two airframes were modified to the XB-47D configuration, chronic shortages of spare parts prevented them from flying regularly. *Ray McPherson*

This short lived nose art on air frame # 51-2103 depicts the cannibalization of aircraft # 51-2046. *Ray McPherson*

"Rascal Missile Carrier," the DB-47B

Several B-47s were modified to carry the Bell GAM-63 missile. Better known as the "Rascal" (Radar Scanning Link), the liquid-fueled GAM-63 was the first guided missile tested by the US Air Force. Bell technicians inspect the GAM-63 prior to a test flight. *Bob Robbins*

The mach 2.95 GAM-63, which was capable of delivering a 3,000-pound warhead nearly 100 miles. Here the ground crew prepares aircraft # 51-5219 for takeoff. *Bob Robbins*

The GAM-63 was suspended from the starboard side of the B-47 fuselage. Once released, the 31-foot missile was controlled from the mother ship. *Bruce Bailey*

Although numerous tests flights were flown with the GAM-63 attached to the B-47, Project Pilot Art Roberts made a single successful attempt to fire the missile in-flight. *Bob Robbins*

"Radar Testbed," the YB-47J

In 1956 a single YB-47J prototype aircraft, a converted B-47E, was used to evaluate the MA-2 radar bomb-navigation system of the B-52. *Jack Martin*

Upon the successful completion of the YB-47J flight test program, fifteen Lockheed built aircraft were converted and assigned to the 44th BW. It is unlikely that any carried the YB-47J designation. Test bed aircraft # 53-2281 is seen taxing at Eglin AFB, Florida, in 1956. *Mike Habermehl*

Project Officer Captain Shaw and Project Engineer Mr. Takayami resting under the nose of the YB-47J prototype at Eglin AFB. *Jack Martin*

"Ma and Pa," the YB-47F and KB-47F

Affectionately known as "Ma" and "Pa" by the aircrews at Wright-Patterson AFB who flew them, two B-47Bs were converted to test probe-and-drogue aerial refueling possibilities in the B-47. A refueling probe was fitted to the nose of the YB-47F receiver aircraft, # 50-069, while the KB-47G tanker aircraft, # 50-040, was fitted with a bomb-bay mounted fuel tank and a retractable hose. Here we see the YB-47F with the rear main landing gear extended in order to increase drag during refueling operations. *Chuck Anderson*

Problems with the B-47 probe-and-drogue in-flight refueling system proved insurmountable and the concept was abandoned in favor of the established flying boom method. On several occasions the refueling hose hung up during the retraction procedure and a crew member was required to cut the hose in order for the tanker to land. *Chuck Anderson*

"The Navy and the B-47," the EB-47E and NB-47E

During the 1960s two B-47Es, aircraft # 24-100 (NUCAR-3) and # 24-120 (NUCAR-4), were bailed to the US Navy for use in fleet electronic warfare testing. Both would remain active long after the last US Air Force B-47 had been retired. *Sigmund Alexander*

A variety of electronic pods containing jamming devices and chafe dispensers were utilized by the B-47 crews during training exercises to test fleet readiness. *David Hall*

A single NB-47E, aircraft # 53-2104, was loaned to the US Navy during the development of the General Electric TF-34 engine. The port side external fuel tank was removed and a pylon installed allowing in-flight engine testing. *Robert Dorr*

"Drones," the QB-47E

Beginning in the late 1950s a series of obsolete B-47s were converted to unmanned radio-controlled drones for use as targets during guided missile testing. This example, a former RB-47E, is painted with high visibility day glow orange panels. *Robert Dorr*

"Foreign Service," the CL-52

The only Stratojet to be flown by a foreign air force was a B-47B, # 51-2059, which was loaned to the Royal Canadian Air Force for use as a flying test bed during the development of the CF-104 Avro Arrow Orenda Iroquois turbojet engine in 1956. *Bob Robbins*

"Proposed 4-Engine Variants," the YB-47C and X-B47

A proposed 4-engine B-47, known as the YB-47C, underwent considerable engineering and wind tunnel work at Boeing. Although the design came too late to meet B-47 production requirements, improvements were to include upgraded Pratt and Whitney J-57 engines and a new, thicker, more efficient wing which was incorporated on the B-52. An artist's conception of the proposed YB-47C model. *Bob Robbins*

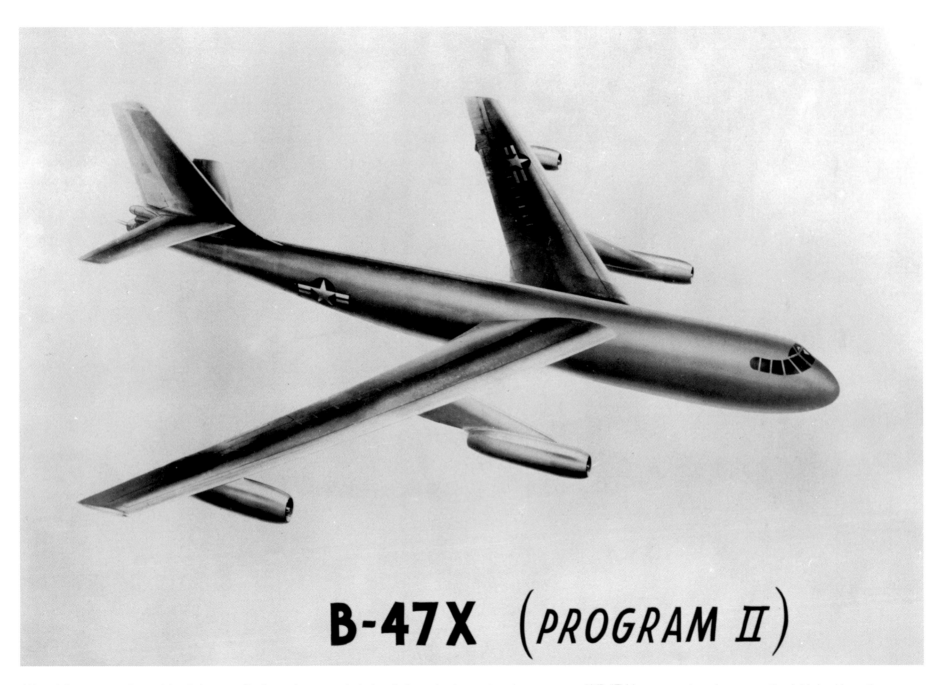

B-47X (PROGRAM II)

Although it never went beyond the design stage, Boeing engineers conducted preliminary development work on a proposed XB-47X. Improvements, such as conventional side by side seating arrangement similar to the B-52, engine upgrades, and increased internal fuel capacity were proposed. Yet another Boeing proposal, the B-47Z, was configured similarly to the X model, but without side by side cockpit, was also rejected. *Bob Robbins*